THE TWELVE SIGNS OF THE 'ULAMA WHO HAVE CONCERN FOR THE HEREAFTER

*An Excerpt from the **Ihya 'Ulum al-Din** of*
IMAM ABU HAMID AL-GHAZALI

Summarized by

MAWLANA MUHAMMAD ZAKARIYYA KANDHALAWI

Translated by

M. TAYYAB BAKHSH BADAYUNI

Editor's note: In his masterpiece, Ihya 'Ulum al-Din, Imam al-Ghazali writes passionately about the evils of not acting on knowledge and the signs of the 'ulama of the hereafter. A condensed version of this lengthy passage was rendered into Urdu by Shaykh al-Hadith Mawlana Muhammad Zakariyya Kandhalawi and produced in part two of Fada'il-i-Sadaqat, which was subsequently translated from Urdu into English by M. Tayyab Bakhsh Badayuni.

These twelve signs have, under the instructions of Dr. Hanif Kamal, been edited and are now being reproduced on Deoband.org; this is primarily for the benefit of the editor, the 'ulama in general, and — since we live in confusing and delicate times — for the general lay populace to allow them to identify the true inheritors of the prophets (peace be upon them).

I pray Allah Most High grants us all, through His divine accordance, the correct understanding of His din, the ability to live according to His noble wishes and desires, and acceptance to serve His din with sincerity.

—Ismaeel Nakhuda.

MAM AL-GHAZALI (MAY ALLAH MERCY HIM) WRITES: An *'alim* who is enamoured of the world is meaner and lower in spiritual status than an ignorant person; he will be punished in the hereafter more severely. Successful indeed are the *'ulama* who have been favoured with nearness to Allah Most High and who are ever concerned about the hereafter. There are certain distinguishing signs of such *'ulama*:

THE FIRST: an *'alim* is one who does not try to acquire wealth through his learning. The lowest of rank among the *'ulama* is one who is fully aware that this material world is despicable, mean, polluted and temporary; and that the life hereafter is vast, everlasting and glorious beyond imagination, the bounties whereof are absolutely pure. Besides, every true *'alim* fully understands that this world and the hereafter are opposed to each other. They are, so to say, like two wives married to one and the same husband — when one is pleased with him, the other is naturally displeased. To give another example, they are like two scales of a balance, when one goes down, the other goes up automatically. Indeed, the present world and the world hereafter are poles apart. They are like two wives of a person — if you seek to get closer to one, it will be at the expense of the other. He who does not realise that this material world is of low value and impure, the pleasures of which are gained at the cost of hardships in this world and in the hereafter, is not of sane mind.

It is a common experience that all worldly joys involve taking pains in this world and unavoidable sufferings in the hereafter. How can a person of such insane mind become an *'alim*? Furthermore, a person who has no idea of the magnificence of the hereafter and its everlastingness is not a believer. How can such a person be an *'alim*? If a person does not realise that this world and the next have opposing interests and wishes to combine both, then he is trying to do something that is undesirable.

Such people are in fact ignorant of the code of life of all of the prophets of Allah Most High. If a person knows all these facts and still gives preference to his worldly interests, he is a slave of Satan, ruined by lusts and facing an evil fate. Such a lost soul cannot, obviously, be counted among the *'ulama*.

Sayyiduna Dawud (peace be upon him) relates that Allah Most High says, "If an *'alim* prefers worldly desires to My love, the least I do to him is that I deprive him of the bliss of having communion with Me, he cannot experience the sublime joys inherent in the remembrance of Allah Most High and in supplications to Him. O Dawud, have no regard for an *'alim* who has been intoxicated by his lust for this world, for he would lead you astray from My love. Such people are robbers. O Dawud, if you find someone who really seeks My countenance, become his servant. O Dawud, if anyone comes to me running, I record his name as a sane wise person and I do not punish such a man."

Yahya bin Mu'adh al-Razi (may Allah mercy him) said, "When knowledge and wisdom are employed for gaining worldly advantages, then they are divested of lustre and glory." Sa'id bin al-Musayyib (may Allah mercy him) said, "If you find an *'alim* remaining constantly with princes, then consider him a thief."

Sayyiduna 'Umar (may Allah be pleased with him) said, "If you find an *'alim* enamoured of this material world, then he must be blameworthy in religious matters, for everybody occupies himself with things which are dear to him."

Someone asked a divine, "Can anyone who takes pleasure in sinful deeds become an *'arif* (a gnostic) of his Lord"? The divine replied, "I can say, without hesitation, that he who prefers this world to the next cannot be an *'arif*; relishing sins is a far greater evil." It should also be borne in mind that no *'alim* can be regarded as one concerned about the hereafter merely due to his rejection of worldly wealth, unless he also has no ambition for worldly honour or status. For these ambitions are more harmful to the soul than the lust for wealth.

In other words, all of those warnings that have been mentioned above about giving preference to the world and seeking it not only include earning wealth but also include even more the seeking of grandeur. This is because the pitfalls and harms of seeking glory are greater than seeking wealth.

THE SECOND distinguishing characteristic of a true *'alim* is that there should be no contradiction between his knowledge and his practice of *din*. He preaches good to others and does not practice himself.

Allah Most High says: *"Do you enjoin righteousness upon others while you ignore your own selves, although you keep reciting the Book?"* (*Al-Baqarah: 44*)

He says elsewhere: *"It is severely hateful in Allah's sight that you say what you do not do."* (*Al-Saff: 3*)

Hatim al-Asam (may Allah mercy him) said, "On the day of Resurrection, none will be more grieved than an *'alim* who imparted knowledge to others which they acted upon and were granted eternal success, while he himself did not act upon his knowledge and, therefore, failed miserably." Ibn Simak (may Allah mercy him) said, "There are many who enjoin *the* remembrance of Allah Most High upon others, but do not remember Him themselves; they admonish others to fear Allah, but they themselves disobey Him most audaciously; they persuade others to cultivate proximity to Allah, but are remote from Him themselves; they invite others unto Allah, but themselves flee from Him."

'Abd al-Rahman Ibn Ghanam (may Allah mercy him) said that ten Companions of the Prophet (may Allah be pleased with them) related to him the *hadith*, "We were once sitting in Masjid Quba and learning (religious) knowledge when the Messenger of Allah (may Allah bless him and grant him peace) came and said to us, 'Acquire as much knowledge as you will but Allah Most High will not reward you unless you act upon what you know.'"

THE THIRD distinguishing characteristic is that he is always concerned with such branches of knowledge that are beneficial for the hereafter and which exhort one to perform good deeds. He is least interested in that branch of knowledge that has no or little use in the hereafter. In our foolishness, we also regard that type of knowledge as *'ilm*, the purpose of which is only earning the world, even though it is sheer ignorance for such a person to consider himself educated [of the religious sciences]; it is then the case that such a person is not particular about learning religious knowledge. An illiterate person, on the other hand, is in the least conscious of his ignorance and therefore tries to acquire religious knowledge. Great indeed is the loss of a man who believes himself to be an *'alim* though he is steeped in (sheer) ignorance.

Hatim al-Asam (may Allah mercy him) was a renowned saint and favourite pupil of Shaqiq al-Balkhi (may Allah mercy him). Once the *shaykh* asked him, "Hatim, how long have you been here in my company?" He replied, "Thirty-three years." The *shaykh* said, "What did you learn during these years from me?" Hatim (may Allah mercy him) replied, "I have learnt eight issues." At this, Shaqiq (may Allah mercy him) out of sheer disappointment recited, "We are surely Allah's and we shall surely return unto him."

He said regretfully, "You learnt only eight lessons during these long years of association with me? I have wasted all my life in associating with you." Hatim (may Allah mercy him) said, "I have learnt only eight lessons — I cannot lie to you". The *shaykh* said, "Tell me, what are those eight lessons?" Hatim (may Allah mercy him) answered:

1] "I have found that everybody loves someone or something (wife, children, property, friends, etc.), but I know that as soon as he is laid in the grave, the loved ones part company with him. Consequently, I have cultivated love for good deeds so that when I do pass into the grave my loved ones accompany me and after death I am not alone." Shaqiq (may Allah mercy him) said, "You have done well."

2] "I have read in the Holy Qur'an that Allah Most High says: *Whereas for the one who feared to stand before his Lord, and restrained his self from the (evil) desire, Paradise will be the abode.'* (Al-Nazi'at: 40-41)

"I know that whatever Allah Most High says is true. Therefore, I have restrained myself from worldly desires until I became steadfast in devotion to Him.

3] "I saw in the world that those things which are most dearest and precious to men are preserved with great care and protected with diligence.

"Then I read in the Qur'an that Allah Most High says: *'What is with you shall perish and what is with Allah shall last.'* (Al-Nahl: 96)

"Accordingly, whenever I came by something which was of great value to me, or which I prized above other things, I consigned it to the custody of Allah (spent it for the cause of Allah Most High), so that it should be preserved forever.

4] "I have observed that (for honour and glory) some men turn to wealth, some to nobility of parentage and others to other things of pride. That is, they take pride in wealth, high parentage etc., and assert their superiority over others.

"But I have read in the Qur'an that Allah Most High says: *'Surely the noblest of you, in Allah's sight, is the one who is most pious of you.'* (Al-Hujarat: 13)

"I have therefore cultivated piety in myself, so that I should become the noblest of men in the sight of Allah Most High.

5] "I have noticed that people upbraid others, revile them or find fault with them. This is all out of jealousy in that one is jealous of the other.

"Then, I read in the Qur'an that Allah Most High says: *We have allocated among them their livelihood in the worldly life, and have raised some of them over others in ranks, so that some of them may put some others to work.'* (Al-Zukhruf: 32) (That is to say, if all men were alike and equal in rank, no one would work for others or serve anybody and, consequently, there would be disorder and chaos in the affairs of the world.)

"Therefore, I have restrained myself from jealousy and ceased to concern myself with other people's affairs. I know for certain that the distribution of livelihood is entirely in the hands of Allah Most High and He grants as much as He pleases to whomsoever He likes. I therefore ceased to harbour enmity against anyone, realising that a man's personal effort has little to do with his prosperity or adversity. It has rather been foreordained by Allah Most High Who is the Sovereign Lord of the worlds. So, I do not feel angry with anyone.

6] "I have observed that nearly everyone in this world is hostile to someone or the other. Having paid attention, I noticed that Allah Most High says in the Qur'an: *'Surely Satan is an enemy for you. So, take him as an enemy.*

He only invites his group (to falsehood) so that they become inmates of the blazing fire.' (Al-Fatir: 6)

"So, I have directed all my hostilities against Satan alone and I try to keep away from him by all possible means. Since Allah Most High has commanded us to treat him as an enemy, I bear no enmity against anyone save Satan.

7] "I have observed that all people are struggling hard to seek livelihood, so much so that they disgrace or abase themselves before others and adopt unlawful means for procuring their daily bread.

"But I have read in the Qur'an that Allah Most High says: *'There is no creature on earth whose sustenance is not undertaken by Allah.' (Hud: 6)*

"Considering that I am also one of the creatures that move on earth whose sustenance depends upon Allah Most High, I occupied myself with paying what I owe to Allah Most High and ceased to worry about what Allah Most High has taken the responsibility to provide.

8] "I have observed that all men have faith upon and put their trust in things which have themselves been created by Allah Most High. Some have faith in their estates or businesses, others in their own craftsmanship, and there are still others who trust their health and strength. In short, all people have put their trust in things that are created like themselves.

"I have read in the Qur'an that Allah Most High says: *'And whoever places his trust in Allah, He is sufficient for him.' (Al-Talaq: 3)*

"I have, therefore, put my trust and faith in Him alone."

Shaqiq (may Allah mercy him) thereupon said, "Hatim, may Allah bless you with *tawfiq* (divine aid for performance for good deeds). I have seen the teachings of the Torah, the Injil, the Zabur and the Holy Qur'an, and I believe that these eight moral lessons form a gist of all that is really good and beneficial for man. Therefore, anyone acting upon these precepts will be deemed to have practised the learning contained in all of the four scriptures revealed by Allah Most High."

Such learning can only be attained by those 'ulama who are really concerned about the hereafter ('ulama al-akhirah). These truths lie too deep for those (so-called) 'ulama who are ambitious for material wealth and who hanker after worldly honour and recognition.

THE FOURTH distinguishing characteristic is that *'ulama* of the hereafter are least interested in the elegance of dress or delicacies of food. Such an *'alim* should, rather, exercise moderation in these matters, and follow the example of his seniors. He should bear in mind that simplicity in dress and food will be helpful to him to advance in nearness to Allah Most High and place him at a high rank among the *'ulama* of the hereafter. Quite relevant here is an amazing episode about Shaykh Hatim al-Asam (may Allah mercy him) narrated by one of his pupils, Shaykh Abu 'Abd Allah al-Khawwas (may Allah mercy him). He relates, "Once, we were with our *shaykh* in a village called Ray. There were three hundred and twenty persons with us and we were all going for the Hajj. We were a group of *mutawakkilin*[1] and we had no provisions or any kind of equipment but had faith in Allah to look after our needs. In the village, we came across an ordinary businessman who, though he looked rather an ascetic person, invited the entire group to dinner and we stayed there for the night.

"The next morning he said to Shaykh Hatim (may Allah mercy him) that he was going to enquire about the health of an *'alim* who was ill, and that the *shaykh* could accompany him if he so wished. Shaykh Hatim (may Allah mercy him) said, 'It is a blessed deed to enquire after an ailing person and visiting an *'alim* is an act of devotion; I would be pleased to accompany you.' This *'alim* was Shaykh Muhammad bin Muqatil, the *qadi* of that area. When Shaykh Hatim (may Allah mercy him) reached his house and saw its magnificence, he was lost in thought. He exclaimed to himself, '*Allahu Akbar!* An *'alim* living in such a tall house?' Anyhow, we requested permission to enter and when we walked in we saw that its interior was most magnificent — neat, clean and spacious, with curtains hanging all round. Shaykh Hatim (may Allah mercy him) gazed upon all these things and began to wonder. Soon we reached the *qadi's* room; he was lying in an extremely soft bed. A slave stood at his head fanning him.

"The businessman made *salam*, sat besides him and enquired about his health. Shaykh Hatim remained standing. The *qadi* motioned him to sit down, but the *shaykh* refused to take a seat. The *qadi* said, 'Have you got anything to say?' The *shaykh* said, 'I want to ask you about a religious

---

1. Sufis who placed their trust (*tawakkul*) in Allah Most High (editor).

matter?' The *qadi* said, 'Say it.' Shaykh Hatim (may Allah mercy him) said, 'Sit up in bed?' At this, the servants helped him and the *qadi* sat up in bed.

"Shaykh Hatim: 'From whom did you acquire your knowledge?'

"*Qadi*: 'I learnt it from the reliable *'ulama*.'

"Shaykh Hatim: 'Who did these *'ulama* learn from?'

"*Qadi*: 'The Companions (may Allah be pleased with them) transmitted it to them.'

"Shaykh Hatim: 'Who imparted it to the Companions?'

"*Qadi*: 'The Messenger of Allah (Allah bless him and grant him peace) imparted it to them.'

"Shaykh Hatim: 'Who conveyed it to the Messenger of Allah (Allah bless him and grant him peace).'

"*Qadi*: 'Jibril (peace be upon him) conveyed it to him.'

"Shaykh Hatim: 'Who revealed it to Jibril (peace be upon him)?'

"*Qadi*: 'Allah Most High revealed it to him.'

"Shaykh Hatim: 'Is there any indication, in the entire body of knowledge revealed by Allah Most High to the Messenger of Allah (Allah bless him and grant him peace) through Jibril (peace be upon him) and transmitted to you through the Companions (may Allah be pleased with them) and reliable *'ulama*, to the effect that the taller a man's house the more exalted he is in the sight of Allah Most High?'

"*Qadi*: 'There is no such indication in that knowledge.'

"Shaykh Hatim: 'If not, what occurs in that body of knowledge?'

"*Qadi*: 'It occurs that, in the sight of Allah Most High, those are exalted to positions of honour who abstain from the world, desire the hereafter, love the poor, and spend for the cause of Allah, thereby treasuring up their charities with Allah Most High for the Hereafter.'

"Shaykh Hatim: 'Then, whose example are you following? Are you following the Sunnah of the Messenger of Allah (Allah bless him and grant him peace)? Are you imitating the Companions (may Allah be pleased with the) and god-fearing *'ulama*? Or, are you following in the footsteps of Fir'awn and Nimrud? O wicked *'alims*. The ignorant people of the world who are enamoured by it say when they see men like you, "If such is the plight of the *'ulama*, then it is normal for us to be worse than them."'

"Saying this, Shaykh Hatim (may Allah mercy him) went away. This severe admonition had a bad effect on the *qadi's* health and he grew worse. There was much talk about this incident and someone told Shaykh Hatim (may Allah mercy him) that Shaykh Tanaffasi (may Allah mercy him), who lives in Qazwin (a city eighty-one miles from Ray) leads an even more luxurious life. So, Shaykh Hatim (may Allah mercy him) set out on a journey to Qazwin with a view to admonishing him. On reaching there, he said, 'I am a man from a non-Arab country. I beseech you to instruct me in *din*, beginning with its rudiments. That is, I would like you to demonstrate to me how *wudu* is performed, for *wudu* is the key to *Salah*.' Tanaffasi said, 'With great pleasure,' and asked someone to fetch water. He then performed *wudu* before the *shaykh* to show him how it is performed.

"Shaykh Hatim (may Allah mercy him) said, 'Allow me to perform *wudu* before you, so that I may learn it properly.' At this, Shaykh Tanaffasi got up and the *shaykh* sat in his place. He began to perform *wudu* and washed his hands four times. Shaykh Tanaffasi said, 'This is extravagance; you should wash every limb thrice only.' At this Shaykh Hatim said, 'Glory to Allah Most High. It is extravagant of me to use a little extra water for *wudu*, but is it not extravagant of you to make use of all these accessories and accoutrements that you possess?' Then, of course, Shaykh Tanaffasi realised that Shaykh Hatim (may Allah mercy him) had not come to learn, but to admonish him.

"After this, Shaykh Hatim (may Allah mercy him) went to Baghdad. When Imam Ahmad bin Hambal (may Allah mercy him) learnt about him and his affairs, he came to see him. The *imam* asked him, 'How can one be safe from the taint of the world?' Shaykh Hatim (may Allah mercy him) replied, 'You cannot protect yourself from the evil influence of the world unless you possess four qualities: you forgive people for their ignorant behaviour towards you, you do not behave towards them in the same manner they behave with you, you spend on others whatever you have, and you do not feel greedy for what other people possess.'

"Later, when Hatim (may Allah mercy him) reached Madinah Munawwarah, people who heard of him, came to see him and gathered around him. He said, 'Which city is this?' The people said, 'It is the city of the Messenger of Allah (may Allah bless him and grant him peace).' Shaykh Hatim said, 'Which is the palace of the Messenger of Allah (may Allah bless him and grant him peace)? I would like to pray two *rak'ahs* in his palace.' They said that the Messenger of Allah (may Allah bless him and grant him peace) did not live in a palace, but in a humble low-roofed house. Shaykh Hatim (may Allah mercy him), 'Show me then the palaces of the Companions (may Allah be pleased with them).' The people said, 'The Companions also had no palaces to live in; they lived in small houses with low roofs a little above the ground.' Shaykh Hatim said, 'Then this must be the city of Fir'awn.' The people seized the *shaykh* and presented him before the ruler (because they thought he was guilty of sacrilege in calling Madinah Munawwarah the city of Fir'awn). When the ruler demanded an explanation, Hatim said, 'Don't be in such a hurry. Listen to what I say till I have finished. I come from a non-Arabic country. When I entered this city, I asked which city it was and they said that it was the city of the Messenger of Allah (may Allah bless him and grant him peace).' The *shaykh* then repeated the entire conversation that had passed between him and the people of Madinah and thereafter recited the following verse from the Qur'an: *There is indeed a good model for you in the Messenger of Allah — for the one who has hope in Allah and the Last Day, and remembers Allah profusely.*' (*Al-Ahzab*: 21) (This verse means that, in all circumstances, one should follow the example of the Messenger of Allah [may Allah bless him and grant him peace]).

"He then said, 'Allah Most High commands us to follow in the footsteps of the Messenger of Allah. Now tell me whether you are following the Sunnah of the Messenger of Allah or the way of Fir'awn?' At this the people released him."

Relating to this, it should be noted that it is not forbidden to enjoy things that are permissible (*mubah*), nor is it unlawful to have an abundance of such things in one's possession. However, the affluence of such luxuries creates a strong liking for them to such an extent that it becomes difficult to do without them. One has to consequently busy himself in providing these things for oneself, and in increasing one's means of income. And, the one who devotes himself to increasing his wealth often adopts a compromising attitude towards his religion. What is worse, such people often commit sinful deeds. If it had been easy to involve oneself in worldly affairs without getting contaminated, the Prophet of Allah (may Allah bless him and grant him peace) would not have so seriously admonished his Ummah to abstain from absorption in worldly pursuits, nor would he have been so personally particular about avoiding worldly taint to the extent that he refused to wear an embroidered robe.

In a letter to Imam Malik bin Anas (may Allah mercy him), Yahya bin Yazid al-Nawfali (may Allah mercy him) wrote, after praising Allah Most High and invoking His choicest blessings on the Prophet of Allah: "I have come to know that you put on fine clothes, take fine bread and sleep in a soft bed. You have also appointed a doorkeeper at your house. All this looks odd, considering that you are one of the great and re-nowned *'ulama* and people come to you from far off places to learn religious knowledge. You are our *imam* and preceptor and people follow your example. I suggest you should be very cautious in these matters. I am submitting these lines merely as a sign of my sincerest regards for you and no one except Allah Most High knows about this letter. The end. *Wa al-salam.*"

In reply to this letter, Imam Malik (may Allah mercy him) wrote: "I received your letter, which contained much advice and admonition for me, besides being a sign of your kindest regard for me. May Allah bless you with piety and righteousness; may Allah grant you the best rewards for this advice; may Allah grant me *tawfiq* (divine aid) to act upon your advice. Indeed, nobody can perform good deeds or protect himself against bad deeds without help and favour from Allah Most High; what you have heard of me is true. I am in the habit of using all these things. May Allah forgive me. However, all these things are permissible under Shari'ah.

Allah Most High says: *'Say, "Who has prohibited the adornment Allah has brought forth for His servants, and the wholesome things of sustenance?" Say, "They are for the believers during this worldly life (though shared by others), while they are purely for them on the day of Resurrection. This is how We elaborate the verses for people who understand."'* (*Al-'Araf*: 32)

"I am fully aware that, notwithstanding their permissibility, it is far better not to make use of these adornments. I should hope that, in future, you would be kind enough to write to me from time to time. I shall also continue to write letters to you. With regards. *Wa al-Salam.*"

Imam Malik (may Allah mercy him) has made a very subtle point. He has given a legal opinion (*fatwa*) about the religious permissibility for using the good things of life and, at the same time, admitted that it is better to abstain from them.

THE FIFTH distinguishing trait of the *'ulama al-akhirah* is that they (without any necessity) keep away from sultans and rulers, and never visit them. Rather, if they do then they keep their meetings short, because their companionship may involve seeking their pleasure and winning their goodwill. Besides, such people are often involved in oppressive and impermissible deeds, the disapproval of which is necessary, along with exposing their oppression and admonishing their sinful deeds. Remaining silent in such matters amounts to compromising one's religion. Furthermore, if one is obliged to praise them with a view to winning their favours, then this amounts to speaking lies; and if one feels inclined towards and a yearning for their wealth, then this is forbidden. In short, associating with them leads to several detrimental issues. The Messenger of Allah (may Allah bless him and grant him peace) said that whosoever lives in the wild becomes hardhearted; the one who is fond of hunting becomes neglectful (of everything else); and the one who visits the kings frequently falls into temptations.

Sayyiduna Huzayfah (may Allah be pleased with him) said, "Beware of the places of temptation." On being asked what they were, he said, "The doors to the houses of princes. Whosoever visits them will have to approve of their misdeeds and (by way of praise) he will have to attribute to them such qualities that they do not possess."

The Messenger of Allah (may Allah bless him and grant him peace) once said that the worst among the *'ulama* are those who visit princes and the best among the princes are those who visit the *'ulama.*

Shaykh Samnun (may Allah mercy him) (one of the companions of Shaykh Sirri al-Saqati [may Allah mercy him]) narrates that if you hear about an *'alim* as being enamoured of the world, consider him at fault in his religion. I experienced it myself. Whenever I went to see the king, on coming back I looked within my heart and found the ill-effects of the visit affecting my soul even though I talk to the kings with severity, contradict their views sternly and do not partake of anything that belongs to them, to the extent that I abstain from even drinking plain water so long as I am with them. Our *'ulama* are worse than the rabbis of the Children of Israel. For they go to the rulers and show them dispensations, and seek to win their favours. If they were to tell the rulers about their responsibilities in plain words, they would feel them a burden and would not like their coming; whereas their truthfulness would be a means of eternal salvation. Indeed, for the *'ulama* to visit rulers is a major *fitnah* and a means of Satan leading them astray, especially in the case of those who can speak eloquently. Satan tells them, "Your visiting them will lead to their rectification, they will refrain from tyranny on account of this and the symbols of Islam (*shi'ar*) will be preserved." Consequently, the said person will believe that visiting them is also an act of religion, though the fact is that visiting them leads one to compromise to win their hearts, and praise them unnecessary, which is fatal to one's *din*.

In a letter to Hasan al-Basri (may Allah mercy him), 'Umar bin 'Abd al-'Aziz (may Allah mercy him) wrote, "Send me the names and addresses of suitable persons whom I should ask to assist me in the affairs of the caliphate." Hasan al-Basri (may Allah mercy him) replied: "The people of religion will not come to you and you will not select worldly people (and, of course, the greedy and avaricious persons should not be entrusted with such tasks, for they will corrupt the affairs of the government). Because of this, I suggest you employ persons of noble descent because their sense of honour will not allow them to tarnish their inherited nobility with dishonest deeds."

This was the reply sent by Hasan al-Basri (may Allah mercy him) to 'Umar bin 'Abd al-'Aziz (may Allah mercy him) whose piety, equity and justice are exemplary, so much so that he is known as the Second 'Umar.

This view is held by Imam al-Ghazali (may Allah mercy him), but this humble author (Shaykh al-Hadith Mawlana Muhammad Zakariyya) feels that unless it becomes necessary to decline such offers for religious reasons, there is no harm in accepting the responsibility (to assist the caliph) in the affairs of the caliphate, provided that one is watchful and capable of protecting one's self. Rather, sometimes, it becomes imperative to accept such responsibilities in the interest of the din or because necessity demands it. However, it is very important that one does not accept such tasks for personal motives, personal interests, material gains or worldly honour and glory. One should, instead, keep in view the needs of the Muslim community.

Allah Most High says: *"Allah knows him who spoils (does not try to improve the lot of the people) from him who improves (the lot of the Muslims)." (Al-Baqarah: 220)*

THE SIXTH distinguishing sign of the *'ulama al-akhirah* is that they do not take hasty decisions when giving verdicts in religious law (*fatwas*) and are very careful in giving advice on religious matters. They refer, as far as possible, cases to someone else whom they consider to be capable of making such decisions.

Shaykh Abu Hafs Nishapuri (may Allah mercy him) says, "A true *'alim* is one who, while giving an opinion in religious matters, is afraid and thinks that he will have to explain, on the Day of Resurrection, the authority on which he had given a decision in such and such a case."

Some of the *'ulama* have said that the Companions (may Allah be pleased with them) would greatly avoid four things:

1. Becoming an *imam* (one who leads the obligatory prayers);
2. The guardianship of a deceased person (i.e. the responsibility to distribute his property according to the will made by him);
3. Accepting a trust;
4. Giving decisions (*fatwas*) in religious matters.

And their five great interests in life were:

1. Reciting the Holy Qur'an;
2. Remaining in the *masjids*;
3. Remembrance of Allah Most High;
4. Enjoining what is good;
5. Forbidding evil.

Ibn Husayn (may Allah mercy him) said, "Some people hurriedly pronounce a decision (*fatwa*) on religious law in such important matters which, if they had been presented to Sayydiuna 'Umar (may Allah be pleased with him), then he would have gathered together all the leading Companions (may Allah be pleased with them) who had participated in the Battle of Badr and consult them."

Sayyiduna Anas (may Allah be pleased with him) is such an illustrious Companion that he spent ten years in the service of the Messenger of Allah (may Allah bless him and grant him peace). Still, whenever he was asked regarding an issue of *fiqh*, he would say, "Ask Mawlana Hasan."[2] (This Hasan al-Basri [may Allah mercy him] was from among the famous jurists, Sufis and Tabi'is.)

When Sayyiduna Ibn 'Abbas (may Allah be pleased with him) (who was an illustrious Companion and was given the title *ra'is al-mufassirin* [Leader of the Commentators of the Qur'an]) would be asked his view, he would direct people to Jabir Ibn Zayd (may Allah mercy him) who was a Tabi'i well versed in issuing *fatwas*. Sayyiduna 'Abd Allah Ibn 'Umar (may Allah be pleased with him), himself an illustrious Companion and a profound scholar of *fiqh*, referred cases to the Tabi'i Sa'id Ibn al-Musayyib (may Allah mercy him).

THE SEVENTH distinguishing characteristic of the *'ulama al-akhirah* is that they are seriously interested in the esoteric science, in other words *Suluk*. They strive greatly in purifying their inner selves and hearts, as this is a means of progressing in the exoteric knowledge. The Messenger of Allah (may Allah bless him and grant him peace) said, "Whosoever acts upon what he knows, Allah Most High will grant him knowledge of that which he has not acquired."

It occurs in the scriptures of previous prophets (peace be upon them): "O children of Israel, say not, knowledge lies in the skies above; who can make it descend upon us? Nor should you say, knowledge lies in the bowels of the earth, too deep for us to dig out. Nor say, knowledge lies

---

2.   The word *mawlana* is used explicitly by Imam al-Ghazali in the Arabic of *Ihya 'Ulum al-Din*. Sayyiduna Anas' (may Allah be pleased with him) usage of the word to describe a man of learning is an early precedent for its use in this context (editor).

across the seas too far away for us to reach it. Knowledge lies within your own hearts. Remain in My presence, observing proper etiquette in the manner of great spiritual beings and cultivate the pious manners of the *siddiqin*; I shall cause knowledge to spring forth from your hearts, so much so that you will be overwhelmed by knowledge." Experience shows that the pious beings who have attained nearness to Allah Most High are granted access to such knowledge and insight which cannot be found in books.

The Messenger of Allah (Allah bless him and grant him peace) said that Allah Most High said, "No means whereby My servant seeks My Favour are more pleasing to Me than the observance of the *fard* actions (such as *Salah, Zakah, Sawm,* Hajj etc.). My servant keeps coming closer to Me with *nafl* actions, until I make him My favourite, and when I make him My favourite, I become his ears with which he hears, his eyes with which he sees, his hands with which he holds, and his feet with which he walks. If he asks Me for something, I fulfil his desire, or if he seeks refuge against anything, I grant him refuge." (*Al-Bukhari*)

Meaning, his walking, seeing, hearing and all actions conform to the pleasure of Allah Most High. Some other versions of the hadith add: "Whosoever despises or bears enmity against any one of my friends has declared war against me."

Since the thoughts and contemplation of the *walis* of Allah are connected to Him, the subtle knowledge of the Holy Qur'an are revealed to them, and its secrets are made clear to them; this is especially the case with those who remain constantly engaged in the *dhikr* and meditation of Allah Most High. And each individual receives from this, with *tawfiq* from Allah Most High, an amount that is equivalent to his concern for good actions and efforts.

In a lengthy *hadith* — quoted by Hafiz Ibn Qayyim (may Allah mercy him) in his book, *Miftah Dar al-Sa'adah* and by Abu Nu'aym (may Allah mercy him) in his book *Al-Hilyah* — Sayyiduna 'Ali (may Allah be pleased with him) is reported to have mentioned the qualities of the *'ulama al-akhirah*. Sayyiduna 'Ali (may Allah be pleased with him) said hearts are like vessels and the best hearts are those that preserve good as much as possible. He also said that gathering knowledge is better than accumulating wealth for knowledge gives you protection while wealth needs your protection, and knowledge increases through use while wealth decreases when spent. The benefits of wealth do not remain after it has been spent, but the benefits of learning are eternal.

He then heaved a deep sigh and said, within my bosom, there is much knowledge. I wish I could find people who would be capable of receiving this knowledge. However, I find those who employ religious pursuits to amass wealth; or I find people who indulge in sensual pleasures, bound by the shackles of following their desires; or involved in amassing worldly wealth.

Anyway, this is a long passage and I (Shaykh al-Hadith Mawlana Muhammad Zakariyya Kandhalwi) have only quoted a portion of it here.

THE EIGHTH distinguishing characteristic is that their faith and belief in Allah Most High is ever increasing and they are always concerned about this — firm belief is [a believer's] capital. The Messenger of Allah (may Allah bless him and grant him peace) said, "Firm belief (*yaqin*) is *iman* in its entirety." He also said, "Learn how to believe truly." The meaning of this *hadith* is that one should diligently sit with those who possess strong belief and follow their example so that, by virtue of their blessed companionship, one can attain perfect faith.

He should have perfect belief in the absolute power and attributes of Allah Most High just like his belief in the existence of the sun and the moon. He should have perfect belief that Allah Most High alone is the doer of all things, all the various material means are under His sole control and He employs these means as He wills. This is like a stick in the hands of a person who beats someone with it, but nobody holds the stick responsible for it. When this belief becomes firmly rooted in the heart, it will become easy for him to cultivate the qualities of *tawakkul* (trusting in Allah alone), *rida* (willing acceptance of what has been decreed by Allah Most High*)* and *taslim* (submission to the supreme will of Allah Most High).

He should also have perfect belief that Allah Most High is the sole individual responsible for providing sustenance (*rizq*), and that He has taken the responsibility for the *rizq* of every individual as has been predetermined; he will, under all circumstances, receive it. That which has not been predetermined will not reach him under any circumstance. When this belief becomes firm, one will exercise moderation in the struggle to earn one's livelihood. Such belief checks greed and avarice and one will not feel grieved if one fails to achieve something.

He should also have firm belief that Allah Most High is watching all deeds, good or bad, at all times; that even an iota small good or bad deed is in the knowledge of Allah Most High; and that reward or punishment will certainly reach him. He should strongly believe that all virtues are rewarded just as he believes that eating bread satisfies one's hunger. Similarly, he should believe that evil has certain consequences, just like the bite of a snake (in short, he should be attracted by good deeds, as a hungry person is by food; and should feel afraid of sins, as he is scared of a snake or a scorpion). When he is firm in this, then he will have complete yearning to perform every type of good deed and total care to refrain from every type of evil deed.

THE NINTH distinguishing characteristic of the *'ulama al-akhirah* is that, under all conditions, they should wear a true expression of being inspired with the fear of Allah Most High. His greatness, magnificence and fear should manifest from their every gesture — from the style of their dress, from their personal habits, from their speech and even from their silence. A mere look at such an *'alim's* face will inspire one with the remembrance of Allah Most High. Calmness, serenity, modesty, and humbleness should have become his manner. He abstains from idle or meaningless talk, and his manner of speaking is natural and unassuming, as this is born of pride and haughtiness, and indicates a lack of fear of Allah Most High. Sayyiduna 'Umar (may Allah be pleased with him) said, "Acquire knowledge, and acquire calmness, proper poise and gentleness for knowledge; behave modestly with those from whom you learn, and let those who learn from you be humble with you. Do not become one of the tyrannical *'ulama* for your knowledge cannot be based on ignorance."

The Messenger of Allah (may Allah bless him and grant him peace) said, "The best of my Ummah are those who in public look happy thinking of the infinite mercy of Allah Most High, but in private weep and cry for fear of His punishment. They are bodily on earth, but their hearts are absorbed in the heavens." Someone asked the Messenger of Allah (may Allah bless him and grant him peace), "Which is the best act of virtue?" He replied, "Abstaining from what is unlawful and keeping your tongue occupied continuously with the *dhikr* of Allah Most High." Someone asked, "Who is the best companion?" He replied, "He who warns you of negligence in good deeds and aides you in performing them." Someone asked, "Who is a bad companion?" The Messenger of Allah (may Allah bless him and grant him peace) replied, "The one who does not warn you when you are negligent in your good actions, nor helps you when you want to do them." Someone asked, "Who is the greatest *'alim*?" He replied, "The one who lives in greatest fear of Allah Most High." Someone asked, "With whom should we associate most frequently?" He replied, "Those who inspire you with the *dhikr* of Allah Most High."

The Messenger of Allah (may Allah bless him and grant him peace) said: "The carefree person in the life Hereafter will be the one who remained concerned in this life; the one who will laugh the most in the Hereafter will be he who wept most in this life (for fear of Allah Most High)."

THE TENTH distinguishing feature of the virtuous *'ulama* is that they are more concerned about those regulations of Islamic law which pertain to religious practices; to what is lawful and unlawful. That is to say, they are interested in actions that it is obligatory to perform and are very keen to know things that are necessary to avoid. Similarly, they are very particular in learning about things that may undo any virtue (for example things which make *Salah* invalid, the virtues of using a *miswak* etc.). They do not indulge in discussions relating to abstruse branches of knowledge for the sake of being regarded as a research scholar, a sage or great philosopher.

THE ELEVENTH distinguishing characteristic of a virtuous *'alim* is that he has studied, with deep insight, various branches of knowledge. He does not accept the opinions of others, for we are bound to follow the Messenger of Allah (may Allah bless him and grant him peace) and seek guidance from his sayings alone. We follow the Companions (may Allah be pleased with them) simply because they closely observed and followed the ways of the Messenger of Allah (may Allah bless him and grant him peace). Since following the *Sunnah* of the Messenger of Allah (may Allah bless him and grant him peace) is of fundamental value, a true *'alim* should be very particular about collecting the *hadiths* of the Messenger of Allah (may Allah bless him and grant him peace) and should make them the object of his serious consideration.

THE TWELFTH distinguishing feature of the *'ulama al-akhirah* is that they are strict and stringent in their avoidance of *bid'ah*. Something becoming a common practice does not means that the thing is a reliable religious practice, for true religion consists in following the *Sunnah* of the Messenger of Allah (may Allah bless him and grant him peace). It should be seen what the Companions (may Allah be pleased with them) did in such matters. Hence, it is imperative to undertake a thorough study of the ways and manners of the Companions (may Allah be pleased with them) and to remain deeply involved in this.

Hasan al-Basri (may Allah mercy him) said: "Two types of person are innovators and they have introduced two kinds of innovations in Islam: [1] He who thinks Islam is that which he understands, and only he who agrees with him will attain paradise, and [2] he who lives a life of comfort and worships the world, he likes those who struggle to achieve worldly things and dislikes those who do not try to earn worldly wealth. Leave both of them alone for the hellfire. As for him whom Allah Most High has protected from these people, he is following the footsteps of the pious predecessors. He has adopted their manners and practices. It is they who will be generously rewarded in the hereafter by Allah Most High."

Sayyiduna 'Abd Allah Ibn Mas'ud (may Allah be pleased with him) said, "Yours is the age in which desires are restrained by (religious) knowledge; a time will soon come when knowledge will be subservient to desires." Meaning people will try to justify whatever pleases their fancy with their knowledge.

Some Divines said, "During the times of the Companions (may Allah be pleased with them), Satan sent forth his detachments to all four corners of the world. They roamed the world and came back, disheartened and exhausted. Satan asked, 'How did you fare?' They said, 'These people (the Companions) worry us. We cannot affect them in any way; we are in great difficulty because of them.' Satan said, 'Don't worry. These people are the Companions of their Prophet (may Allah bless him and grant him peace); influencing them is difficult. Soon, you will have people who will do what you desire.' Then, once again, Satan sent forth his detachments in all directions during the times of the Followers (Tabi'in). Satan's disciples again came back, worn out and cast down. When he asked them how they fared, they said, 'They annoyed us; they are a strange people. During the day, we do succeed to a certain extent in tempting them. But as soon as the evening falls, they repent of their sins so sincerely that all our labours are lost.' Satan again said, 'Don't worry. A time is soon coming when people will behave in a manner most pleasing to you. They will follow their own desires, taking them to be a religious duty. They will not think of repentance; they will rather give religious sanction to their irreligiousness.' After some time, Satan introduced into Islam such innovations, which were accepted as a part of religion. How could they possibly repent from such sins when they believed themselves to be on the right path?"

This is a brief account of the twelve distinguishing characteristics of the virtuous *'ulama* that have been thoroughly discussed by Imam al-Ghazali (may Allah mercy him). The *'ulama* should, therefore, particularly fear the Day of Reckoning because their reckoning will be severe and they have a greater responsibility. The Day of Resurrection, the day on which this reckoning will take place, is a difficult day. May Allah Most High, in His Infinite bounty and mercy, protect us all from the severity of that day.